About the A

Lucy Leadbeater

Lucy was a student at the Gymnasium Münchenstein in Basel, Switzerland, in 2022 and as part of her studies she was required to write a 20,000-word research paper on a subject of her choice.

Her mother was born and raised on the island of Guernsey and during family visits there, Lucy had often heard her grandmother and her great-aunt talking about the occupation of the island by German forces during the Second World War and about their own evacuation to England to escape it.

She, therefore, decided to focus her dissertation on the reliability of oral history in the context of those older relatives recalling their wartime experiences some eighty years later.

Lucy's paper earned her very high marks, with the examiners commenting that it was a very interesting and moving piece of work.

Neil Robin

Neil has lived in Guernsey for all of his life and worked for the Guernsey civil service for thirty years, then another twelve years in journalism and public relations before retiring in 2019.

Neil is married with two children and five grandchildren and spent the first couple of years of his retirement writing a couple of books – namely *A Breed Apart* (published by Pegasus) and *Cobo Sunset*.

As an old family friend, Neil asked if he could read a copy of Lucy's paper and on doing so, he felt sure that it could be the basis for a good book.

Neil and Lucy agreed that while there had been a good number of books written about the occupation of the Channel Islands during the Second World War, there seemed to be rather less written about the experiences of the child evacuees.

This prompted them to press ahead with the idea of recording the wartime memories of Lucy's elderly relatives in a book, together with brief reminiscences from eight other child evacuees, so that these might be informative to and enjoyed by future generations.

Neil, therefore, set aside completing *Cobo Sunset* and turned his hand to translating Lucy's academic piece accordingly. The collaboration of Neil's creative writing skills and Lucy's research work has resulted in what you are currently holding in your hand. We hope you enjoy it.

A Home from Home

Lucy Leadbeater and Neil Robin

A Home from Home

Vanguard Press

Dedication

The two people to whom this book should primarily be dedicated are the two main characters herein – namely, Lucy's grandmother, Betty Le Gallez, and her great aunt, Kathy Ferbrache.

When Lucy sat down with them in 2022 to chat about their evacuation experiences, Betty (above right) was eighty-eight years of age and Kathy (above left) was ninety-two. Both of them still quite sprightly and both still very much retaining 'all of their marbles'!

Sadly though, Kathy passed away in October 2023, just before this book was published.

This book is also dedicated to Lucy's father, Andy Leadbeater, who passed away in 2015.

Prologue

For readers who may not be familiar with the island of Guernsey, the following may help to provide an understanding of the place itself, of the events leading up to its occupation by German forces between 1940 and 1945 and the evacuation of a significant portion of its population at the beginning of that time.

Guernsey is the second largest of the Channel Islands (the others being Jersey, Alderney, Sark and Herm, plus a handful of smaller uninhabited islands), which form an archipelago situated in the English Channel and lying in the shelter of the Bay of St Malo.

Although the islands switched allegiance from France to the English Crown in 1204, their geographical position (less than fifteen miles from the French coast but more than seventy-five miles from the English coast) has seen many families, places and roads continuing to bear French names.

That geographical position also meant that the islands were of significant strategic military value, as forces based there were able to observe and fire upon any enemy vessels and later aircraft that passed close to them.

Included in the deal for the Channel Islands to become part of England in 1204, King John had undertaken to maintain a military presence in both Guernsey and Jersey in order to protect them from any subsequent attempt by the French to regain them.

In Guernsey, a military camp was established at a site to become known as Fort George, and British soldiers continued to be stationed on the island for the next seven hundred and thirty-five years as a deterrent to any would-be invaders.

Guernsey comprises of ten parishes and up until the 1960s, each of them had its own primary school: St Andrew, St Martin, Forest, Torteval, St Pierre du Bois, St Saviour, Castel, Vale, St Sampson and St Peter Port.

The latter was the most densely populated parish, and so had two primary schools, Amherst and Vauvert. There were also two Catholic primary schools on the island, plus a couple of private schools for children of the well-heeled.

Prior to the Second World War, there were two single-sex intermediate schools (later to be re-named the Grammar School for Boys and Grammar School for Girls), to which the more academically-inclined were able to progress, but the majority of Guernsey's early-teens found themselves entering the world of employment at that relatively tender age.

Chapter 1

On the south-east tip of Guernsey lies an area known as Icart Point and this was the home of the Roberts family in the few years prior to World War Two.

They lived in a delightful Victorian property called Icart, sitting at the top of steep cliffs and providing the base for a simple and happy life in the late 1930s – albeit against the backdrop of increasing unrest in mainland Europe.

In the spring of 1940, the family comprised of Harold Roberts and his wife Kathleen, together with their three daughters, Kathy, Betty and Doreen. The two older girls attended St Martin's parish school, but Doreen was just a babe-in-arms and so remained at home with her mother.

About five years earlier, the Roberts family had been living in small rented accommodation in the neighbouring parish of St Andrew and at that time there were only three of them. But, with Kathy at four years of age and another baby on the way, it was clear that a larger home was going to be needed.

Harold's mother lived a tiny cottage a couple of miles away, just above Saints Bay, and she had come to learn of a gentleman who had recently arrived in Guernsey from Canada with the intention of buying a property and settling on the island.

The man had duly bought the house called Icart, just

along the road from her cottage, and he was now looking to employ a 'live-in' couple as housekeeper and gardener to look after his sizeable property.

When the family came to visit her the following weekend, Harold's mother told him about this opportunity and, after a quick discussion about it with his wife, he strolled along the road to Icart and knocked on the front door.

It was opened by the new proprietor, Adolphus John Saunders and after Harold had introduced himself and explained the reason for his visit, he was invited inside. The two men sat in comfy armchairs beside the inglenook fireplace and began to discuss the matter at hand.

Although he had initially been thinking of employing an older and childless couple, within a short time of their conversation Mr Saunders soon warmed to the quiet, sensible and affable personality of the applicant currently sitting before him.

Mr Saunders also reasoned to himself that it really was rather a large house and, while he had envisaged giving over only a drawing room and a bedroom to his housekeeper and gardener, there would still be another bedroom standing empty and so it would therefore not be a big deal to have the couple's children sleeping in there.

Also, despite his own childless status, Mr Saunders had always been very fond of children and he soon warmed to the idea of having this young family living in his home.

He duly offered the gardener and housekeeper jobs to Harold, even though he had not even met Kathleen, and

Harold readily accepted without even thinking to discuss remuneration!

Harold returned to his mother's cottage to happily share the news with his heavily-pregnant wife and their daughter that they were soon to move to a new home. A couple of weeks later, their possessions were loaded onto a cart and the little family set off to begin their new life.

Harold and Kathleen's second daughter, Betty, was born soon after they moved into Icart and a strong bond soon developed between the Roberts family and Mr Saunders. This closeness was to become epitomised by a nickname for him which became used by the whole family and which was happily embraced by the man himself.

The nickname came about due to the fact that Mr Saunders almost invariably wore a hat, indoors and outdoors in summer and winter, it was very rare to see him without it. The girls even wondered if he wore it in bed at night!

As a toddler, Betty found it difficult to say 'Mr Saunders' and so started to call him 'Man in Hat'. Kathy took this up, but dropped the final word and then somehow it became 'Manon'. Before long, all of the family were calling him by that nickname – once they realised that he didn't mind at all.

The immediate vicinity around Icart provided the girls with plenty of fun and adventures, with fields in which to run and play – at the end of which was the top of the cliffs, where they could peer over the 200-feet drop to the beach below.

They could then scramble down the rough paths and

make-shift steps to go for a swim in the warm waters below, explore the rock pools and enjoy many hours playing on the sand.

The relationship between Manon and the little girls effectively saw them adopting him as an honorary grandfather and enjoying cuddles and getting treats from him – all of which were perfectly innocent and caused their parents no concern whatsoever.

There was just one occasion when the happy relationship was briefly strained though. Manon had asked Harold and Kathleen if he could take Kathy and Betty on the bus to St Peter Port so that he might introduce them to the joys of a matinee performance at the island's cinema.

Of course, this was the days of black and white 'slapstick' films featuring the likes of Charlie Chaplin, Buster Keaton and the Keystone Cops. However, not long into the film, a four-year-old Betty decided she didn't like it much and began complaining that she wanted to go home.

Manon and Kathy were both enjoying it though, so he simply told Betty, "If you don't like it, you can go and wait outside." And the headstrong wee girl duly decided to do just that.

However, to his horror on leaving the cinema after the end of the film, Manon could not find Betty anywhere. Eventually, he and Kathy gave up the search and caught the bus back to Icart Point to face the music from Harold and Kathleen.

Imagine their relief therefore, when they entered the house and saw Betty happily sitting with her parents! Just a few words of concern about what had happened were exchanged between the two men out of earshot of the girls, but that was about it – as both of them saw the funny side of the four-year-old getting on the bus from town unaccompanied and making her own way home! They assumed that the bus-driver had also been amused and had let her off paying the fare accordingly, as she had no money on her.

'Manon' Saunders in his ever-present hat.

Such was the extent to which Manon had embraced them as his own family that when Harold and Kathleen told him that a third child was on the way, he suggested that an extra room needed to be built on the back of "their" section of the house – and he and Harold duly built it together.

The Roberts sisters spent a very happy few years living at Icart and had no reason to think that this blissful state of affairs would not continue for many more years to come. However, their parents and Manon and many other adults living in Guernsey at the time were becoming increasingly aware of and very concerned by the situation unfolding in mainland Europe.

Chapter 2

Adolf Hitler and his Nazi Party had come to power in Germany in 1933 and had spent the next few years building their country's military might, so that it had the largest army, navy and air force of any European nation, together with the largest stockpile of weapons.

A 'friendly' annexation of Austria enhanced the Nazi power-base, but they soon decided to expand their empire still further by invading Poland on 1 September 1939 – thereby precipitating a declaration of war against Germany by Britain and its allies two days later, after Herr Hitler had ignored their demand to immediately withdraw his troops from Poland.

Undeterred by the increased resistance to their expansion, German forces proceeded to make inroads into other neighbouring countries, firstly northwards into Denmark and Norway, then south and west into The Netherlands, Luxemburg and Belgium.

The British Government considered it unlikely that the Nazis would dare to invade another large European country and so believed that the German forces would desist their southward advance once they reached the French border.

To back up this assumption, Britain withdrew its military presence based in the Channel Islands and redeployed them to support the protection of the northern regions of France.

Up until this point, the people of Guernsey had perhaps taken some comfort from the fact that the hostilities were taking place quite some distance away, but the removal of the British garrison from their island brought home the realisation that the German forces could soon get even nearer and possibly even invade.

"The British stopped The Hun in their tracks in northern France in the last war in Europe, so there's no reason to think they can't do the same again this time," Manon reasoned when discussing the situation with Harold. "I know a lot of men died in the trenches back then, but at least it stopped the Germans getting anywhere near Guernsey."

Unfortunately, Manon's attempt to put a positive spin on things proved ill-founded as, despite the reinforcement of defences on the French border, German forces did not abort any attempt to advance well into French territory. They proceeded apace through France over the ensuing couple of weeks – in a period in history that became known as Blitzkrieg.

British and allied forces were totally overpowered, precipitating Operation Dynamo – the evacuation of around 340,000 of them from the French port of Dunkirk. This involved a flotilla of small boats joining the large naval vessels plying their way back and forth across the English Channel between 26 May and 6 June 1940 to bring the battered and defeated troops to safety.

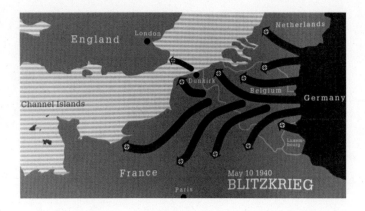

It was at this point that the realisation really began to dawn on Channel Islands residents that the German forces were almost on their doorstep and that the peaceful existence they enjoyed could soon be in grave danger.

Back at Icart, while Harold and Kathleen Roberts and 'Manon' Saunders were acutely aware of the dreadful scenario unfolding just across a narrow strip of water from them, they tried to go about their daily lives as normally as possible in order to protect the three young girls in the household from becoming too fearful.

The evacuation of troops at Dunkirk, together with a message from the UK Government that it could no longer guarantee the safety of Channel Island residents and offering to evacuate them to the British mainland if they wished to leave their island homes, all meant that the authorities within the islands were on the verge of making the most momentous of decisions.

That decision was finally forced upon them on 18 June 1940 when islanders looked to the east and saw that the sky was turning black. This was because the French coastal town of Cherbourg was ablaze!

"Blimey, what's that?" Kathy exclaimed as she pointed to the blackening sky that was clearly visible from the vantage point of Icart high on the cliffs. While their parents were acutely aware of what it meant, they made up a story about a big storm brewing over France rather than risk scaring their daughters too much with the truth.

Chapter 3

The Bailiff of Guernsey, the head of the island's government and judiciary, called a meeting of the head teachers of all of the island's schools that evening – to advise them that they would be responsible for overseeing the evacuation of the pupils in their charge.

The Bailiff and his team had already arranged with the UK Government for the secondment of a number of vessels of varying sizes, some of which had only recently been involved in the evacuation of troops from Dunkirk.

The following day, a notice appeared in the island's

newspaper advising the population of this development and giving them only a few hours to make the necessary preparations.

The newspaper article also went on to advise that mothers with under-school-age children could also go to the UK, while men who were of appropriate age to sign-up in the British forces were also encouraged to escape the island while there was still time.

It was a walk of about one mile from Icart to St Martin's School, a journey that Kathleen would make twice a day, with the two older girls skipping along happily beside her as she wheeled Doreen in the pram there and back.

That walk and arrival at the school on the morning of 19 June 1940 was not really different from any other morning, as the mothers and children were unaware of the meeting between the Bailiff and the head-teachers on the previous evening or of the announcement that was to appear in the newspaper that day.

However, it was a very different story when they gathered again to collect their children from school that afternoon. There were mothers crying and hugging each other and agreeing to meet at the harbour the following morning to try to ensure that they could stay together during the voyage to the mainland.

The children had all been told during the day by their teachers that this was to be the last day that they would all be together at the school for quite some time. Some assumed that it would be no longer than the usual month or so duration of the summer holidays, although a few of the older ones like Kathy, realised that it was something rather different this time.

The children were given a list to hand to their mothers, which itemised the few things that they should pack to take with them on the journey to England the following day.

Children should take with them on evacuation the following articles:-

Gas masks.
2 ration books (current and new one).

Besides the clothes which the child will be wearing, which should include an overcoat or mackintosh, a complete change of clothing should be carried. The following is suggested:-

Girls	Boys
One vest or combinations.	One vest.
One pair of knickers.	One shirt with collar.
One bodice.	One pair of pants.
One petticoat.	One pullover or jersey.
Two pairs of stockings.	One pair of knickers.
Handkerchiefs.	Handkerchiefs.
Slip and blouse.	Two pairs of socks or
Cardigan.	stockings.

Additional for all
Night attire; comb; towel; soap; face-cloth; tooth-brush; and, if possible, boots and shoes and plimsolls.

Blankets must not be taken.

Rations for the journey: Sandwiches (egg or cheese); Packets of nuts and seedless raisins; Dry biscuits (with little packets of cheese); Barley sugar (rather than chocolate); Apple, Orange.

The close-knit Roberts family, including Manon, were devastated by the developments unfolding before their eyes in the space of just a couple of days – as were hundreds of other families across the island.

Harold and Kathleen discussed what might lie ahead for them and their children and, rather than simply ending up wherever the authorities opted to send them, they resolved to take advantage of the fact that they had family

25

connections in Birmingham.

Kathleen was born and raised in Birmingham and, with unemployment rife in the late 1920s, she had successfully answered an advertisement in the local newspaper seeking waitresses to work in a hotel in Guernsey. She duly met and married Harold and they happily continued to live in the island and to raise their family there.

Now though, suddenly, they had to consider life away from Guernsey and they decided that a return to Birmingham for Kathleen, together with their three little girls, was the best option for the female members of the household.

In accordance with the directions contained in the announcement in the newspaper, it was clear and that Harold would have to sign-up to serve in the British armed forces, while Manon would not be able to leave Guernsey with them.

"Well, it's all right for you girls going off on holiday, isn't it?" Manon tried to make light of the situation to try to keep the children from getting upset. "I'll be left here to manage this place all on my own while you lot are all off enjoying yourselves!"

The girls were still a little disappointed that they would be going away without their 'adopted grandfather,' but this was tempered by the excitement and anticipation of travelling off the island on a big ship.

Kathy had left the island only once before, when she was four years of age and her parents took her to visit her maternal grandmother in Birmingham, while Betty had never done so.

Harold and Kathleen decided to set off for the harbour fairly early the following morning with the pram and their few items of luggage, as it was a three-mile walk from Icart Point to St Peter Port and they wanted to be near the front of the queue for the boat to ensure that they got away.

However, as they made their way down the hill to the seafront, they were shocked to see that thousands of other people had had the same idea and had arrived at the harbour even earlier than them. There was just a sea of bodies ahead of them and all they could do was wait while the authorities tried to organise the chaotic situation before them.

Eventually, a message was relayed through the crowd, advising that there would be room for school-age children and teachers only on the handful of boats moored at the harbour that day and that parents and younger children would need to return the following day to try to get on one of the boats then.

Imagine the enormous distress suddenly thrust upon Harold and Kathleen Roberts, and all of the other parents, as they were suddenly told that they had to say goodbye to their children.

"You're the oldest, so I'm relying on you to look after Betty. Hold her hand tightly and don't let her go wandering off," Kathleen tearfully told Kathy. "We'll get on a boat tomorrow and catch up with you in England."

Harold and Kathleen watched as their two small girls pushed their way through the crowd and disappeared from view, before turning the pram around and making the walk back to Icart to tell Manon what had happened.

Chapter 4

The ship that Kathy and Betty boarded was called the *SS Viking* and along with pupils from St Martin's School, there were also children from St Andrew's School and the Forest School.

The promise to hold on to Betty's hand proved impossible for Kathy to keep as, once they were aboard the vessel, the children were separated into their respective school and class groups. Kathy's class was taken to one end of the vessel, while Betty's class was taken to the other end.

The SS Viking

The *SS Viking* was completely packed, with every

cabin, corner and space filled with children and teachers. The journey from Guernsey to Weymouth took around six hours and for most of the children it was not a pleasant experience in that confined space.

Firstly, as it was a balmy June day in Guernsey when they left, most of them were wearing summer clothes and had only packed what had been included on the list that they were given by their schools, which did not include jumpers and coats. As a result, many of them were quite under-dressed for the coldness of the cross-Channel voyage and felt very chilly.

Also, during their long wait to board the vessel, many of the children had already eaten their complete ration of food that their parents had packed for them. On being made aware of this, the captain of the SS *Viking* ordered that the provisions kept in the lifeboats should be broken out and distributed among the children.

Another issue that affected Betty and her class was that they were allocated a section of the ship that on its previous voyage had been occupied by cattle. It had been a swift turn-around after unloading that cargo and so there had been no time to clean that area of the ship before sailing to Guernsey.

There was therefore quite a pungent stench which, along with the fact that the sea was quite choppy, caused many of the younger children to feel sick as they were crammed together in an area where only a little fresh air was filtering through.

Aware that Betty had not been a very good sailor on the odd occasions that she had been out on Manon's fishing boat, Kathy had sneaked a couple of cracker biscuits into her pocket before they left Icart that morning and she gave them to Betty as they boarded the ship and told her to eat them if she started feeling sick.

Unfortunately, the smell of vomit from other children soon negated the binding effect of the crackers and Betty succumbed to an impressive bout of projectile sea-sickness along with most of the rest of them.

There was sadly one fatality aboard the ship during that voyage to England. An eleven-year-old girl called Sylvia Burford had undergone a tonsillectomy operation only a few days before the evacuation. She became very unwell during the crossing and tragically died just before the ship docked in Weymouth.

Midway across the English Channel, the captain and crew saw a number of German planes swooping over the ship and were fearful that they would be fired upon. However, it would seem that the German pilots saw that the ship was full of children and they flew away.

Weymouth was the designated first port of entry for the evacuation vessels and arrangements were in place there to process the men, women and children arriving there from the Channel Islands.

After leaving the ships, the evacuees were taken to large halls where they were served with jam sandwiches and cold tea, had their details taken and given a brief medical inspection.

It was at this stage that some of their luggage went missing. They had to leave their suitcases on the quay while being taken care of in the halls and these were either stolen of somehow otherwise went astray.

Betty was one of the children who never saw her belongings again, but that may have been partly her own fault. After disembarking the ship, her class was made to wait on the quayside for ages and, being a small girl, she became bored and decided to entertain herself by peeling the label off her suitcase!

The sisters were at least able to reunite once they were inside one of the large halls, as they were able to move around more freely than had been possible on the ship. However, Kathy wasn't too keen to honour the promise to her mother to hold Betty's hand, as her little sister was filthy dirty and not smelling too pleasant, having spent six hours sitting in a space previously occupied by a herd of cows and now covered in vomit!

As it was a town located on the south coast of England, Weymouth was within easy reach of German bombers and so the authorities considered it too risky to keep the thousands of evacuees in that area for too long.

The Channel Islanders were therefore loaded onto northbound trains and most of them ended up in towns in Lancashire and Yorkshire, such as Bradford, Bury, Leeds, Manchester, Oldham, Stockport, Wigan and York. A small contingent also continued up to Glasgow.

Chapter 5

Back in Guernsey, Kathleen was distraught as they explained to Manon what had happened at the harbour, but he had been able to calm her a little by reassuring her that she would be able to reunite with her precious daughters within twenty-four hours if they set off for the harbour again even earlier tomorrow.

Harold, Kathleen and Doreen, therefore, commenced the walk to the harbour in near darkness in the early hours of the next morning and were indeed able to get on board one of the boats to England. On arrival in Weymouth though, they frantically tried to ascertain where Kathy and Betty had been sent, but were again distraught when their enquiries came to nothing.

They sat down with a cup of tea and tried to compose themselves and to think rationally about what to do next. They eventually decided to follow their original plan to travel up to Birmingham, where Kathleen and Doreen would stay and Harold would enlist in the armed forces. Kathleen would then have a base from which to continue to try to track down Kathy and Betty.

The Roberts family was just a small part of a huge overall picture that, in the space of two days on 20 and 21 June 1940, saw a total of nearly twenty thousand men, women and children making the voyage across the English

Channel from Guernsey to arrive in the port of Weymouth – of whom around five thousand were children whose parents had chosen to or been forced to remain in their island home.

On the scheduled third day of the evacuation from Guernsey, the German air force bombed St Peter Port harbour, causing such damage that it was impossible for any more people to get away and thereby compelling many to no choice but to await the inevitable invasion.

A few daring souls decided to load their families into small fishing boats and set sail for England. Fortunately, this was happening in the summer months and so the seas were not as treacherous as might have been the case at any other time of the year.

A week after the bombing of the harbour, on 30 June 1940, German troops landed on Guernsey and so began the occupation of the island that would keep many parents and children apart for five years.

The children on board trains heading to the north of England were quite oblivious to what was happening back in their island home as they were absorbed in this new adventure. The experience of even seeing a train, let alone climbing inside one and travelling in it, was quite alien to most of them, as there were no trains on any of the Channel Islands.

The evacuees were given no idea of where they were going on the trains and, as each station they went through had its name blacked out, there were also no clues along the way. They were nevertheless quite excited that from the train windows they could see things that they'd never seen before, such as industrial chimneys, miles of rolling hills and black and white cows!

Town Council officials and volunteers were on hand at the destination stations to greet the evacuees and take them to public buildings such as town halls, dance halls and church halls, which had been transformed into Evacuee Reception Centres.

Kathy and Betty were eventually told to disembark the train when it stopped at one station and they learned there that they were in Stockport. However, they were then separated again as the children were divided into age groups, with the older ones, including Kathy, taken to the town hall and the younger ones, including Betty, taken to a nearby church hall.

There were rows upon rows of mattresses laid out on the floors of these buildings and all of the children were finally able to grab a few hours of sleep after what had been a long and at times frightening twenty-four hours or so for them.

These buildings were to become home for some of the evacuees for anything up to four weeks as the search took place for host families to accommodate them.

Initially, it had been hoped that this would be voluntary, but it had been underestimated just how many Channel Island evacuees would arrive in the UK. The government therefore had to introduce a payment scheme whereby local householders who accepted evacuees into their homes would receive a billeting allowance.

Vans drove up and down the streets of towns, with a loud-speaker telling local people about the Billeting Allowance Scheme. Those who were willing to provide a home for evacuees were invited to go to the buildings where they were being temporarily accommodated and were then granted the choice of who they wanted to take in.

It was a scenario reminiscent of the slave markets in ancient Rome and clearly rather a humiliating process for some of the children to go through – much worse than waiting to be picked for a sports team at school!

Unfortunately, it was not possible to find a host family who were willing to take both Kathy and Betty together and so again the young sisters were separated, resulting in very different outcomes.

Betty was chosen first when the Farrington sisters attended the chapel where she was staying and took to her as soon as they saw her. They were both middle-aged spinsters and had it in mind that they could cope with two girls of around five or six years of age.

They were told that Betty had a ten-year-old sister and that it would be nice to keep the two of them together, but the Farrington sisters were reluctant to take on the responsibility of a girl approaching puberty and they instead opted to take another younger girl from Betty's class, whose name was Margaret.

As Betty had lost all of her clothes on the quayside in Weymouth and had spent the ensuing week or so wearing the same outfit, the first thing the Farrington sisters did was to buy her a number of new items of clothing. This was a new concept for Betty, as she had been used to receiving Kathy's hand-me-downs back in Guernsey!

The Farrington sisters had chosen Betty and Margaret before the inducement of the Billeting Allowance Scheme was introduced and it was clear that their intentions were honourable as they were very kind to the two little girls, buying them toys and showering them with affection.

Kathy's experience was very different though. She was chosen by a family named Pratt, who had answered the call only after the Billeting Allowance Scheme had been announced and it soon became clear to her that not only were they looking for little more than an unpaid home-help and child-minder, but also that they were pleased that they were being paid for that privilege.

The Pratts had a two-year-old daughter called Norma, to whom Kathy was expected to read once she had completed her designated household chores and to generally keep the toddler entertained. Hence, while Betty was quite content with her billet, Kathy was very unsettled with hers and knew that something would have to change.

Chapter 6

The two girls were registered to attend different schools and so were not able to see each other during the week. However, the Farrington sisters and the Pratt family lived fairly near to each other and attended the same church, so Kathy and Betty were at least able to see each other there once a week.

Such was Kathy's unhappiness at the prospect of living with the Pratt family for the foreseeable future that she soon hatched an escape plan and needed to enlist Betty's help to bring it to fruition.

She took her little sister to one side after the service one Sunday and told her that she was going to send a letter to their grandmother's address in Birmingham to see if they could go to live there. Although Kathy had visited there only once and was four years of age at the time, she had somehow memorised the address – which was 43, Harborne Park Road.

"I don't want to go anywhere else; I'm happy here," Betty protested. "They took me to the country this week to see little rabbits playing and they're always doing nice things like that for me and Margaret."

"But Mum said we were all going to live together in Birmingham," Kathy reminded her. "That's probably

39

where her, Dad and Doreen are now, so we need to go there too."

Despite Betty's protests, Kathy managed to persuade her to ask the Farrington sisters for a sheet of writing paper and an envelope and stamp. They were happy to provide these in the belief that the girls just wanted to let their grandmother know that they were safe and well.

Betty gave the notepaper and stamped envelope to Kathy on the following Sunday and once she was safely in bed that night and unlikely to be interrupted by the Pratts, Kathy wrote the letter to her grandmother and posted it on the walk to school the following morning.

When it arrived at the address in Birmingham though, Harold, Kathleen and Doreen were no longer living there. Harold had enlisted in the Royal Navy and been posted to a base on the Yorkshire coast, so his wife and youngest daughter had moved to Bradford to be nearer to him.

They had been unsuccessful in ascertaining any news on where their two eldest daughters had gone and had sadly resigned themselves to not seeing the girls again until the war was over and they might all be reunited again back in Guernsey.

However, Kathleen's mother forwarded Kathy's letter to her in Bradford and finally she was aware of where her girls were living. Kathleen immediately made arrangements for someone to look after Doreen and she jumped on the next train to Stockport.

Imagine Kathy's delight when her mother arrived at the Pratt's house and informed them that she was taking her daughter back to Bradford with her. They showed some disappointment, but that was undoubtedly far more to do with the loss of the billeting allowance payments and the loss of a free housemaid than anything to do with sorrow at the departure of the young girl herself.

There was a very different reaction when Kathleen and Kathy arrived at the Farrington's house to collect Betty though. Although she was pleased to see her mother, Betty was very much enjoying having her own new clothes and toys and treats and expressed her reluctance to go elsewhere.

"I'm very happy here, Mum," she said. "Can't I just stay here and you can visit me?"

"Do you know how difficult and expensive it is to come on the train from Bradford?" Kathleen snapped. "You belong with your real family and that's where you're going to be."

The Farrington sisters were equally saddened that they were set to lose the small girl that they had quickly grown to love so much, but Kathleen was absolutely adamant and they had to accept that it was only right and proper that Betty should be with her mother.

The little girl also had to accept that resistance was futile and she trudged off in tears to put her belongings into a case. Kathleen thanked the Farrington sisters for their kindness to her daughter and then had to practically drag Betty from their house and off to the train station.

Although the Farrington sisters noted Kathleen's address in Bradford and promised Betty that they would write to her, they never did so and she never heard from them again. After a short while, she just assumed that they had forgotten about her and were now devoting all of their kindness and affection towards Margaret, or perhaps that they had taken in another little girl to replace her.

Now reunited in Bradford, Kathleen was faced with the problem of finding accommodation for her family. Her landlady, Mrs Jowett, had been happy to take in a single mother and one child, but when her tenant then turned up with two more children, it was clearly an issue.

Kathleen and Doreen had occupied one single-bedded room in the house, while Mr and Mrs Jowett had their bedroom and their son, Ian, had the other single room. It was obvious that Kathleen and her three children could not share one single bed, while the extra demand on the toilet and cooking facilities was also clearly going to be a major problem.

Harold had also been able to stay over on his occasional nights off from the navy base, but again this was no longer going to be possible either and so they were forced to try to find alternative accommodation nearby.

However, while there were a good number of local householders who were willing to take in one or two evacuees, especially if they could collect payment through the Billeting Allowance Scheme for doing so, there were unfortunately very few of them who had the capacity or inclination to take in a family of five.

It soon became clear that the Roberts family had little chance of being able to stay together if they remained in Bradford and so, with a very heavy heart, Harold agreed that Kathleen and the children should return to her mother's house in Birmingham.

Mr Jowett took them to the train station in his car and they boarded a train for Birmingham, where it soon became evident that they were going to experience the dreadful consequences of the war far more acutely than if they had stayed up north.

This was because Birmingham was one of the main targets for the German air force to drop bombs on an almost nightly basis, thereby causing enormous damage to the city and terror to its residents. Many householders had installed air-raid shelters in their gardens to try to protect themselves from the bombs.

These were called Anderson Shelters and generally comprised of a hole in the ground with a corrugated iron roof over them, which in some cases may not have actually provided very effective protection against harm to life and limb.

The shelter in Kathleen's mother's garden had been built to accommodate only four people and prior to the Roberts girls arriving, she had shared it with her neighbour Mrs Wright and her two children, Danny and Eileen. Mr Wright was away serving in the Royal Air Force.

However, living next door on the other side of her house was a family of five, comprising Mr and Mrs Wotham and their three sons. They had built a large and effective shelter in their garden – into which they were happy to welcome the three Roberts girls.

It therefore became normal practice for the three sisters to spend nights in the Wotham's shelter while their mother and grandmother stayed in their shelter with the

Wright family.

However, Kathleen wanted to ensure that her daughters had extra protection while they were out of her sight and so she bought three metal pudding basins from Woolworths and insisted that the girls wore them on their heads while they slept in next door's shelter.

Chapter 7

Kathy and Betty were enrolled at St Peter's School in Birmingham and Kathy became good friends with a girl called Hazel, with whom she would remain pen-pals for many years after the war had ended.

Betty befriended a girl called Olive, who had arrived there at about the same time as them and with her head completely shaved. Her strange appearance led to her being shunned and teased by the other children, but Betty felt an empathy with her as she too was something of an outsider among the local kids. Unfortunately, the reason for the head-shaving became all too apparent all too quickly, as Betty soon contracted nits!

After overnight bombing raids had finished, it became a bit of a hobby for Kathy and Betty to emerge from the Wotham's shelter and run the short distance to nearby Lordswood Road, which seemed to be an area to bear the brunt of much of the bombing. Here, they were able to collect various bits of shrapnel and other debris left after the pounding of the night before.

However, they only stayed in Birmingham for about six months, largely because Kathleen was growing increasingly concerned about the incessant heavy bombing of the city and also because she was missing her husband terribly.

She had remained in touch with Mrs Jowett in Bradford and was delighted to learn from her that a council house would soon become available which would be able to accommodate her and her three daughters.

Kathleen immediately contacted the council-appointed landlady of that property, Mrs Clancy, and it was agreed that they could move into the house a few days later. Their grandmother was understandably very disappointed that their time with her had been so brief, but she fully accepted that they would be much safer in Bradford than they would in Birmingham.

Kathy and Betty were also disappointed that they were saying goodbye to their friends Hazel and Olive and they solemnly exchanged contact details with promises to keep in touch with each other forever more.

On arrival in Bradford a few days later though, all was not as it had seemed because they discovered that Mrs Clancy was already letting rooms in the house to two other Guernsey mothers and their four children.

It was a two-up, two-down terraced house and Mrs Clancy used the downstairs living room as a bedsit for herself, while the two Guernsey families had a bedroom each upstairs. They all shared the kitchen, which doubled up as a bathroom with the children being plonked in the sink for their baths.

Kathleen was concerned that she had been lured there under false pretences and that Mrs Clancy was planning to cram them in with the other two families. However, Mrs Clancy reassured her that she was in fact moving out to live elsewhere and that the Roberts family would be taking over her room on the ground floor.

This still meant that all four of them would be sleeping together in one room, and five of them when Harold was able to visit, but at least it was a good-sized room and a lot more comfortable than having to try to sleep in an Anderson Shelter and listening to bombs falling nearby.

Kathy and Betty were enrolled in a new school, Hanson High School for Girls, although Kathleen was a little dismayed to learn that all of the pupils there had to wear a uniform.

She had spent most of her money on the deposit and first month's rent for their room in the house and so there was little money left over for school uniforms, at least until Harold's wages from the navy came through to their bank account.

The school's headmistress was called Miss Shulter, who the girls suspected was German given her surname, and she was very understanding about Kathleen's financial situation and arranged for Kathy and Betty to be kitted out with second-hand uniforms for the time being.

Unfortunately, these uniforms were both too big for them and also rather worn and tatty, so the girls felt rather conspicuous among their rather more smartly turned-out schoolmates.

The other two mothers in the house, who the Roberts girls knew as Auntie Sybil and Auntie Eva, were accommodated there under the Billeting Allowance Scheme as their husbands had been unable to be evacuated with them and were still in Guernsey.

47

After a few weeks of all living there together, the three mothers were informed that Mrs Clancy was no longer their landlady and that one of them would need to replace her if they wished to remain in the house.

The council informed them that, as Kathleen was the only one who had a husband contributing to the rent, she was their preferred candidate to become responsible for the property and she duly attended the town hall to complete the paperwork.

At least the return to Bradford would finally provide some sort of stability for the two young girls who had been torn from their happy and peaceful lives on a small island in the English Channel. They had spent a few weeks living with strangers in Stockport, then a few days reunited with their mother and baby sister in one room in Bradford and then six months at their grandmother's house in Birmingham, sheltering from bombing raids almost every night.

Although the house in Bradford was rather cramped with three families living there, it was to be their home for the next four years and also a place of happiness and safety for them as there was not a single air-raid on Bradford during that entire time.

Kathy, Betty and Doreen living happily in Bradford

Chapter 8

Overall, the local communities in the northern towns were very generous to the evacuees, not only by providing them with somewhere to live, either voluntarily or through the Billeting Allowance Scheme, but also in other ways.

Guernsey child evacuees were often gifted books and toys from local children and some shopkeepers even reduced prices for the evacuee mothers. Sometimes, when local people encountered child evacuees on the streets, they gave them money to buy sweets and they were also granted free entry to public activities such as a visit to the cinema, to a football match, to concerts and to the local swimming baths.

However, it did take a while for both parties to get used to these new combined communities, with some locals knowing very little about the Channel Islands and so not even sure that the evacuees could speak English or that they had the same beliefs and way of life as their own.

One example was when the Women's Voluntary Service hosted a function for the evacuees in a church hall. The Guernsey children were rather bemused when these ladies waved greetings and began to gesticulate that they could eat and drink the refreshments laid out on the tables.

The penny then dropped that the ladies of the WVS were under the impression that everyone from Guernsey spoke French and so would not understand if they spoke English to them!

Kathy was even taken aback at school one day when another pupil in the playground shouted at her, "If you're from an island, how come you're not wearing a grass skirt?"

Guernsey's geographical position and genetic links to France did mean that the indigenous population did have a particular accent and their pronunciation of some English words was rather different from the Yorkshire brogue of most of the residents of the evacuees' host towns.

However, this different way of speaking was often a blessing as, on hearing it, many of the local shopkeepers and ordinary townsfolk would immediately offer the afore-mentioned acts of kindness towards the evacuees.

To try to assist the integration of the two communities, a number of so-called 'Channel Island Societies' were formed. These were groups of both local residents and Guernsey people who held meetings, raised funds and organised social events such as dances, card games, raffles and Christmas parties for the children.

Kathleen took her children to two such 'clubs' on alternate Saturdays; one was called Saint Havens and the other was called Eastbrook. Getting together with other people from their home island was a tonic for them all, as they chatted about places and events that they recalled from happier times.

There were rarely many men attending these functions, as they were either serving in the armed forces or were left behind in Guernsey, but the women and children still managed to have a very enjoyable time dancing and chatting together.

One Christmas party for the Channel Islands evacuees was held at Eastbrook in December 1941 and was featured in the Bradford newspaper, with Kathleen and Doreen appearing in the accompanying photograph (they are in the bottom right-hand corner).

CHRISTMAS PARTY FOR CHANNEL ISLANDERS.

One thing that was commonplace whenever the evacuated Guernsey folk got together for a social event was a rousing rendition of the Guernsey 'national anthem' and, once they had learned the words, it was something that all three Roberts girls enjoyed belting out with the best of them:

Sarnia Cherie, gem of the sea,
Land of my childhood, my heart longs for thee,

Your voice calls me ever, forget thee I'll never,
Island of beauty, Sarnia Cherie.

Nb. 'Sarnia' was a name given to the island by invading Roman forces on their way to conquer England a couple of thousand years earlier, while 'Cherie' is a derivative of the French word for 'dear' or 'darling.'

Chapter 9

While the evacuees were striving to make the best of living in northern towns far from their island home, most of them yearned for the day when they would be able to return to Guernsey and be reunited with family and friends there once again.

Two major events during this time hugely raised their spirits in that regard: firstly, the Americans entering the war in Europe and secondly, the D-Day Landings.

The United States of America had stayed out of the war for more than two years, but then, on 7 December 1941, its naval base at Pearl Harbour near Honolulu in Hawaii was attacked by Japanese war planes, causing significant loss of life and ships.

America declared war on Japan three days later and then, as Germany and Italy had a pact with Japan, they in turn declared war on America the following day.

The news that a huge nation like America, with the massive military might at its disposal, was joining the Allied forces in Europe was a real boost to the morale of everyone living in Britain, local residents and evacuees alike.

However, it was to be another couple of years before that increased strength in the Allies resources translated into significant progress into mainland Europe and starting to gain the upper hand over the German forces there.

On 6 June 1944, the American general in charge, Dwight Eisenhower, gave the order to launch what was to become known as the D-Day Landings. Hundreds of thousands of Allied troops and supporting military hardware were transported across the English Channel and landed on a number of beaches on the northwest coast of France.

This heralded the start of the drive to push the German forces out of the occupied countries and back into their own territory. This was to take almost another year, but each news bulletin on the radio reporting Allied progress was greeted with mounting excitement as people began to see that the end of the war was in sight.

The news report that probably gained the loudest cheer, other than the one announcing the German surrender and the end of the war, was one on 2 May 1945 telling the news that Adolf Hitler had committed suicide in a bunker in Berlin the previous day.

Six days later, in a speech on the radio at three p.m. on 8 May 1945, the British prime minister, Winston Churchill, announced the end of the Second World War in Europe and, to the great delight of the evacuees and their families back in Guernsey, his speech also included the words "…and our dear Channel Islands are also to be freed today."

While the German troops stationed in Guernsey did lay down their arms on the 8 May, it was the following day before a platoon of British soldiers stepped ashore and officially liberated the island from German rule.

The 9 May of every year since has been a public holiday in Guernsey, with islanders displaying Union Jack flags and bunting on their houses, staging a cavalcade around island roads, holding street parties and other events to mark and celebrate their Liberation Day.

For many Guernsey residents who had remained on the island throughout the German occupation, the most visual proof that it was safely back under British protection was when King George VI and Queen Elizabeth visited the island on 7 June 1945.

However, the island was not instantly ready for the return of thousands of evacuees, as much had changed in the five years while they had been away.

With so many properties left empty by the fleeing evacuees, the senior German officers did not need to concern themselves with building barracks in which to house their troops. They simply commandeered any empty houses that suited their needs and sadly the occupants of those properties during the ensuing five years did not keep them clean or maintain them.

The Germans also commandeered some properties that were not empty if they were deemed to be of strategic advantage and Icart was one of those. Given its position on top of the south coast cliffs, it afforded an excellent vantage point from which the Germans could keep watch, not only for a possible invasion of the island but also to look out for Allied military vessels that might be heading to inflict damage on German positions along the French coast.

This meant that Manon was unceremoniously ousted from his home, but he was fortunate that a neighbour invited him to live in an unoccupied dower wing on the side of their farmhouse.

The Germans then took out the downstairs windows of Icart and sealed up the holes with concrete blocks, while they also replaced the wooden front and back doors with heavy iron ones to create a fairly impregnable watchtower.

Other watchtowers were created at roughly half-mile intervals right around the island's coastline, although much of the work had already been done for the Germans, as Martello towers had been built around one hundred and sixty years earlier by the British in order to deter the French from trying to re-take the island.

The Martello towers were built from local granite and the Germans added concrete extensions to them and, at points around the coast where there were no Martello towers, such as Pleinmont and L'Eree, they built huge concrete watchtowers of their own.

German watchtower at L'Eree

Concrete gun emplacements and bunkers were also constructed all over the island, along with deep trenches and minefields, and so it was a very different place for the returning evacuees from that which they had left five years before.

Chapter 10

Back in Bradford, like some of the evacuees in other towns, some of the Guernsey folk were not looking forward to their return to their island home. Some of them had secure jobs and lodgings, their children were settled at school and good friends had been made. Therefore, quite a number declined the opportunity to return and instead opted to stay and continue their lives on the UK mainland.

A priority order was drawn up for those who definitely did want to move back to Guernsey and this meant another upheaval for Kathleen and her three girls.

As their husbands had remained in Guernsey throughout, Auntie Sybil and Auntie Eva and their children were granted places among the first wave of evacuees to return, but as Harold was in England and had been able to visit his family on his days-off, the Roberts family were placed further down on the list.

Having lived so closely with Auntie Sybil and Auntie Eva and their children for almost five years, Kathleen and her three daughters were sad to see them go, but they were also very excited that their own turn would be coming soon.

Without the Billeting Allowance for the other two women and their children though, Harold's pay was not enough to meet the rent on the house and this meant that Kathleen had to pack up the clothes and the few possessions that they had and take her three daughters back to her mother's house in Birmingham.

A couple of months or so later, Harold was de-mobbed from the navy and was able to join his family in Birmingham. A few days later, a letter came through advising them that they should make their way to an assembly point in London and from there they would be transported back to Guernsey.

The Roberts sisters could hardly contain their excitement as they boarded the train to London and met up there with other Guernsey families arriving from other places in the UK. They were then herded onto other trains taking them to south coast towns such as Portsmouth, Southampton and Weymouth, from where ships sailed them across the English Channel and back to Guernsey.

As their vessels approached the island, the evacuees could see some of the huge fortifications that had been built by the Germans in their absence. Disembarking at the harbour in St Peter Port, they could see that the town itself had not changed too much, but as they then made their way out to the more rural area of the island, they could see just how much of it had been spoiled by the occupying forces.

Icart Point was an area that the Germans had fortified in the event of a raid by Allied forces and, in addition to the bunkers and gun emplacements, they had dug a labyrinth of trenches, which admittedly did provide Betty and Doreen with an exciting new playground in the weeks and months to come.

As telephone communications had been re-established between Guernsey and the UK fairly swiftly after the liberation of the island on 9 May, Manon had been able to forewarn Harold that, because of what the Germans had done to it, Icart was not yet fit for habitation by the young family.

Therefore, when they did return to the island in early September, the Roberts family made their way to Harold's mother's cottage and they cuddled up together in one room for their first night's sleep back in Guernsey.

They made their way to Icart the following day and were stunned to see the state of it following the departure of the German soldiers who had lived in it for five years.

Not only had the ground floor windows been blocked up and iron doors installed, but a large iron stove had been placed in the middle of the kitchen, with a make-shift flue from the top of it running across to the fireplace and away up the chimney.

The size and weight of this stove was such that the wooden floorboards could not have coped and the Germans had therefore ripped these out, leaving the kitchen with a floor consisting of no more than ground and rubble.

A further shock was in store for Kathy when she ran to the nearby farmhouse where Manon had been living since he had been turned out of his own home by the Germans. She knocked on the door and it was opened by Manon, but he didn't recognise her.

Kathy had been a ten-year-old little girl when she left Guernsey, but was now a fifteen-year-old young woman and she had to tell Manon who she was. Kathy wanted him to grab her and give her a big cuddle, but Manon refrained from doing so and just told her how lovely it was to see her again.

Betty had a similar experience later in the day when she and Harold were waiting at the bus stop to go into town. Manon came walking along the road and he warmly shook hands with Harold but simply greeted Betty verbally and with no physical contact.

Manon and the girls had enjoyed cuddles when they were small, but either he felt that it was inappropriate now that they were older or his affection for them had waned during the five years since they had last been together.

Chapter 11

While most of the German personnel were shipped away from Guernsey in the months following the liberation of the island, a few hundred were kept behind to help with clearing the minefields and dismantling the gun emplacements and other installations.

However, the concrete watchtowers and bunkers were so solidly built that it would have required major blasting operations to get rid of them and so they have remained intact ever since and probably will continue to do so for many years to come.

While the majority of the German soldiers had treated the local population well during their occupation of Guernsey and often gave the children sweets and other treats, fraternising with them was largely frowned upon by most of the locals remaining on-island during those years.

However, most Guernsey people also recognised that most of the German soldiers were not Nazis and were just ordinary young men with families of their own at home and that many of them actually had no great desire to be part of the Nazis' intrusion into other countries.

Manon and Harold set to work with sledgehammers, knocking out the concrete blocks that had sealed up the downstairs windows of Icart and they were allocated a couple of German soldiers to help them with this task.

Kathy was now of an age when she was becoming interested in boys and the two German lads were only a few years older than her. Rudi and Karl both had blond hair and blue eyes and Kathy thought they were the most handsome boys she had ever seen.

Although her parents told her to have nothing to do with the German boys or she would be in big trouble, Kathy and a couple of her friends thought there could be no harm in just sitting nearby and watching the two young men as they went about their work.

It wasn't long before Kathy's two friends plucked up the courage to go over and engage in conversation with the German lads, but Kathy refrained from doing so as she was too scared that her father would see her.

The two girls became good friends with Rudi and Karl and while their relationships remained strictly platonic, they exchanged addresses when the boys were due to leave Guernsey and they all remained pen-pals for many years thereafter.

Once Icart had been restored to its former glory, with new windows and doors, the removal of the German stove and re-laid floorboards, Manon and the Roberts family were able to move back into the house and resume the happy lifestyle that they had enjoyed before the war.

As they got to know each other again after the five-year break, Manon and the girls soon rebuilt the bond that they had previously enjoyed and he again became the 'honorary grandfather' that he had been when they were younger.

In the years to come, Kathy, Betty and Doreen would

all grow up, get married and move away from Icart into homes of their own, where they raised their own families. Harold and Kathleen continued to live there with Manon for some years, until the old man died and they inherited the house from him.

Many years later, Betty and her husband and their two children moved into Icart, to live with the recently-widowed Kathleen, thus enabling her to again live in the house that had provided her with such a happy childhood.

While our story has concentrated on the experience of one family, it must not be forgotten that thousands of other Guernsey people have stories to tell about their experiences during the Second World War.

Unlike the three Roberts girls, who had spent the war years with their mother and with frequent visits from their father, many other children returned to Guernsey to reunite with parents they had not seen for five years.

Doing so was no doubt easier said than done, with some parents not recognising their own children and struggling to rebuild relationships with them, as their offspring had developed their own personalities, likes and beliefs while living apart from them.

Some children had left behind older siblings who were perhaps in their late teens in 1940 but who had grown into adults, got married and had small children of their own by 1945.

Many others who were just toddlers when they were evacuated from Guernsey only knew about living in a large town with busy streets, trains and factories. For them to adjust to the more peaceful and rural lifestyle of Guernsey proved a lot more difficult for some than for others.

Some children also returned to find that new siblings had been born during the occupation and that their parents seemed to have more of a bond with those new little brothers and sisters than with themselves.

All that said, of course, most of the evacuees quickly settled back into life in Guernsey and successfully devoted themselves to the task of getting to know their family members again and building a new life for themselves back on their home island. However, the psychological impact on all of them of their experiences during the years of the Second World War may well have remained with many of them for many years.

Also not to be forgotten was the kindness of the people of those towns in northern England, who had welcomed thousands of refugees from the Channel Islands and helped them to settle and integrate into their communities.

A contingent of more than one hundred people from Guernsey and Jersey had been transported to the Yorkshire town of Brighouse, between Halifax and Huddersfield, where they soon formed The Brighouse Channel Islands Society and met together regularly throughout the war years to enjoy parties, dances, bingo and other social events.

When came the time for them to leave Brighouse and return to their island homes in 1945, the Society presented the town's mayor with a certificate expressing their gratitude for the kindness and hospitality that they had been afforded over the previous five years.

The certificate was hand-drawn by S H Francis and depicted Channel Island scenes, such as Creux Harbour in Sark, and views in Alderney, Guernsey and Jersey, surrounding a central message of thanks.

Chapter 12

At the time of writing this book in 2023, given that the evacuation of Guernsey residents took place eighty-three years earlier in 1940, it is unlikely that anybody under the age of eighty-six years would be able to recall events surrounding the actual evacuation itself.

Meanwhile, it is likely that only those over the age of eighty years in 2023 would have memories of living in the northern towns of England and a few in Scotland during the war years.

It is therefore, important that stories such as that of the Roberts family are written down and preserved so that future generations can learn and understand what the child evacuees had to go through all those years ago.

We are extremely grateful to have been provided with some memories recalled by eight other child evacuees:

Joan Le Poidevin

Joan was just three years of age and not yet at school when she was evacuated along with her parents and her brother. The family ended up in a village called Tickhill near Doncaster.

One of her earliest memories there is of her mother making 'rag mats' from old trousers and coats donated by the village chapel congregation so that the children would not have to step onto a cold floor when they got out of bed.

She recalls that when she started Tickhill Infants School she was issued with a gas-mask and remembers the children being sent to an air-raid shelter when German aircraft flew overhead on their way to bomb Sheffield steelworks.

Joan's father worked long hours on a farm near the village and the Le Poidevin family were very grateful for the kindness shown to them by the villagers and remained good friends with some of them for many years after the war ended.

When Joan got married and moved into her first home with her new husband, the happy couple even named their house Tickhill.

Bill Robilliard

Bill was nine years of age and attending Amherst Junior School. His parents opted to stay in Guernsey but wanted their only child to escape to a safer place.

Bill was in a contingent of children who continued up to Glasgow, but after a short while there he was sent to live with an uncle in Sutton, a small town just outside London.

It was an unhappy time for him though, as he was abused both physically and psychologically by his uncle during the five years he had to live there.

One consolation for lacking the parental care enjoyed by other children in the area though, was that Bill was often first on the scene to collect shrapnel, which was a lucrative commodity when it came to bartering at school!

One of the events that Bill witnessed during his first few months in Sutton in 1940 was the Battle of Britain, with dog-fights raging between British and German aircraft in the skies over southern England.

Ernie Le Gallez

Ernie was eight years old and attending Amherst Junior School. He was the youngest in a family of ten, but only he and one sister were of school age and so able to be evacuated, while the rest of the family stayed in Guernsey. Ernie and his sister ended up in different parts of the UK and had no contact with each other during the war years. Ernie also travelled to Glasgow with the contingent from Amherst School, where the Robertson family gave him a home.

While they treated him well, the Robertsons were quite strict with Ernie and he was expected to carry out tasks such as bringing in the coal and gardening. Nevertheless, Ernie enjoyed his time in Glasgow and was a little reluctant to leave at the end of the war.

Indeed, when he disembarked at the harbour in Guernsey and saw a group of people waving at him and calling his name, Ernie did not recognise them as his family. It took him quite a while to settle back into island life and he even considered moving back to Scotland.

Ernie kept in contact with his Glasgow family throughout the rest of his life and, five years after returning home, he met and married Betty Roberts and they later spent more than thirty years living in the house at Icart Point.

Derek Le Vasseur

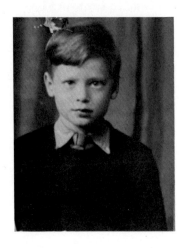

Derek was nine years of age and attending Notre Dame du Rosaire Catholic School. He and his six year old sister, Barbara, were evacuated to a small town called Tottington, near Bury, where they attended Hollymount Convent School.

When they first arrived in England, they and their schoolmates, along with children from another couple of schools, were taken to spend the night in a cinema. Derek had been told by his parents to hold tightly to his sister's hand during the journey, but when he woke up in the cinema in the morning, Barbara was nowhere to be seen.

He learned that she had mistakenly been moved elsewhere with another school, but they were reunited a couple of weeks later when she was brought to be with him in Tottington.

Margaret Burton

Margaret was five years of age and attending St Martin's School. She was evacuated with her mother and her sister, Rose. Her father could not leave the island on the same day as them, but he was able to follow a couple of days later.

The family spent the war years in a town called Morley, which was between Leeds and Wakefield, where they were able to get a council house and the girls attended Robin Hood School in nearby Rothwell.

Their father was above the age-limit to enlist in the armed forces and so he worked in a munitions factory by day and joined the Home Guard for the evenings and weekends.

Gordon Tostevin

Gordon was nine years of age and attending St Peter's School. He and his sister, Rona, were evacuated to Baildon in Yorkshire, while their parents and one brother stayed in Guernsey and their two older brothers enlisted to serve in the armed forces.

When their contingent got to Baildon, the girls were taken to one church hall and the boys to another and then local people were invited to choose a child to be billeted with them.

A childless couple, Mr and Mrs Pratt, decided that they would like to look after both a girl and a boy. Mrs Pratt went to the girls' church hall to choose a little girl and Mr Pratt went to the boys' church hall to choose a boy.

What a remarkable coincidence then unfolded when they got their respective choices home and discovered that he had chosen Gordon and she had chosen Rona, both quite unaware that they were brother and sister!

Gordon attended the Albert Road Junior School and then the Salts Grammar School and he and Rona lived a comfortable and happy life with the Pratts in Baildon, where they were visited by their older brothers whenever they were back in England on leave.

At the end of the war, Rona returned to Guernsey, but Gordon had started an engineering apprenticeship and so he remained living with the Pratts.

It wasn't until 1954 that Gordon finally decided to return to Guernsey and, unable to bear the thought of losing him, the Pratts sold their house in Baildon and bought one in Guernsey!

George Langlois

(No photo available)

George was eleven years of age and attending the Boys' Intermediate School. He can remember him and his schoolmates walking down St Julian's Avenue to the harbour and boarding a Dutch cargo ship, where they were all put in the hold for the overnight sailing to England.

They travelled up to Oldham and spent two or three days in a large room over a Co-op shop before being billeted to live with families there. It was not a particularly happy time for George and he does not to remember much about his host family or the school he attended.

He left school as soon as he could, at fourteen years of age, and moved to Lynwood Manor near Market Rasen in Lincolnshire with three other Guernsey lads, where they got jobs growing parsley.

A short time later, George learned that a Guernsey family he knew were living in Leicester and so he moved there to live with them. He got a job working as a gardener and helping to look after a few animals for a lady who lived in the nearby village of Burton Overy.

This is where George continued to live and work for the remaining two years of the war until he was able to return to Guernsey.

Len Giles

(No photo available)

Len was thirteen years of age when he joined the evacuation party from the Vale School and ended up in Wigan. He was joined a short while later by his parents, three sisters, and two brothers, and the family moved to live in Brighouse.

They set up a home at 117 Bradford Road, which was near Wellholme Park and Len recalls playing there with his younger siblings. However, having turned fourteen years of age and rather than attend school in the UK, Len got a job in a bakery and later worked at Atkinson's Mill.

The family returned to Guernsey in 1945, but Len found it difficult to settle and opted to return to Brighouse, where he met and married Betty and they started a family. They did finally settle in Guernsey in 1964 when Len returned to take over the running of the family greenhouses after his father died.

Conclusion:

As stated earlier, the vast majority of child evacuees from Guernsey were well-treated by their UK hosts. However, it is sad to note that of our cohort of ten of them in this book, two have recalled some level of abuse or maltreatment and another two found themselves billeted with rather strict hosts.

If this number was extrapolated across the five thousand unaccompanied child evacuees from Guernsey, it would suggest that quite a number of them did not have a particularly happy time during this pivotal period in their young lives.

Note:

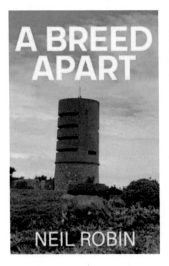 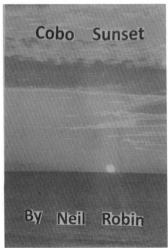

Neil Robin's first book, *A Breed Apart*, tells the story of how both the First World War and the Second World War impacted one Guernsey family. Copies of the book are available from leading bookstores and also online from Amazon or www.pegasuspublishers.com

Neil hopes to complete his next book, *Cobo Sunset*, in the near future.